Dedicated to JOHN & JOAN

My first Brittany was out of a litter advertised in the Seattle Times Classifieds in 1964.

I had been hunting pheasant for years with a Lab in Eastern Washington. The Columbia River's Wanapum Dam and Priest Rapid Dam had recently been completed to provide power to run irrigation circles east between the river and Moses Lake. The Columbia Basin Project produced crops—mostly alfalfa, corn and sugar beets— and pheasant. They were everywhere, with sage brush to roost and food on the ground. My lab kept busting birds 100 yards and more in front of me...It was time to get a pointing dog.

i

Dual Ch. Tigar's Jocko, a Brittany from California, owned, bred and handled by John Munson, had just won the 1964 American Brittany Club's National Amateur Championship in Carbondale, IL. Jocko had also earlier won the PHEASANT SHOOTING DOG CHAMPIONSHIP in California. Jocko's win was the first ever major win by a Brittany against the long tails—pointers and setters.

My father died suddenly in 1967 at age 53. Joann's father died shortly after, which necessitated John and Joann moving to Seattle to run their family magazine-distributing business.

I purchased a Jocko pup from the Seattle breeder and my life changed. The next thing you know, I was obsessed with Brittanys and field trialing as a way to keep my bird dogs in shape during the off-hunting season. In the process, I met John and Joann at Camp Adair in Oregon. It was not long after meeting them that I unofficially adopted them; they filled a real void in my family. John and Jocko's ashes are now scattered on the field trial grounds of Camp Adair.

John also owned Tennessee Walkers (a preferred smooth-riding horse breed used for running bird dog field trials). I learned, trained, trialed and hunted with John and set a personal goal of winning the "Nationals".

John was the wisest, soft spoken man I have ever met...To make a point, he would talk using short, concise sentences...aphorisms. Everything John said had a specific meaning based on his experience. He was born in Arkansas; grew up during the depression; worked his way west; and served on Guam in the Pacific during WWII. Over time, everyone around John began to recognize and use Johnny's "Hip-pocket sayings".

John was a frugal, yet generous man. He introduced me to the concept of the "HIP-POCKET NATIONAL BANK". He had worked hard all his life. He believed if you wanted something you had to work and save for it. He was fond of saying, *"You want to double your money? Then fold it, and put it your hip-pocket."*

Ken Jacobson & John Munson re-purposing Tigar's Jocko's
PHEASANT SHOOTING DOG CHAMPIONSHIP Trophy
for the <u>Pacific Coast Shooting Dog Championships</u>
DERBY CHAMPIONSHIP, a National Championship qualifying stake.
The trophy is now retired at the NATIONAL BIRD DOG MUSEUM.

Ken Jacobson - Author

Hall of Fame National American & Canadian
Dual Ch. Pacolet Cheyenne Sam
NATIONAL BIRD DOG MUSEUM – Grand Junction, TN

I have collected creative communication, "one-liners" or "plays on words" for as long as I can remember, including, sayings, advertising slogans, aphorisms, and oxymorons, as well as graphic logos. I like to create "new" words and concepts. I am fascinated by cattle brands; Yogisms; codes; Mensa; international symbols; Braille; hieroglyphics; petroglyphs; foreign languages—their characters, alphabets and writing; the Annanaki; crop circles; alien markings; and the Peruvian Plains of Nasca. I have great admiration for anyone who can creatively communicate using as few words or symbols as possible.

I had received a football and baseball scholarship at the "U" and was intent on a major league baseball career as a pitcher. Then I was hired by *Industrial Artists,* a technical/patent commercial art studio. Two years later I purchased the firm from its owner, who took the position as lead illustrator at Seattle's largest Patent Attorney firm. I changed the name of the art studio to reflect a new business direction, *Industrial Artists / Creative Graphics,* which later evolved into *Jacobson Advertising,* a full-service advertising agency with fifty employees.

I chose a duck-billed platypus as my agency's logo, stating: *"The Platypus symbolizes our <u>Uniqueness</u>, <u>Versatility</u>, <u>Originality</u>, and <u>Creativity</u>, yet we aren't above laying an occasional egg."*

The 60's and 70's were a period of incredible growth for both television and radio. One the most exciting growth periods at the agency was the creation of broadcast media advertising using a visual graphics background.

Television and radio provide limited 30- and 60-second periods to communicate and sell an idea. Radio is theatre of the mind. It was like being given a new blank medium and then being asked to create visual/mind radio concepts. My test was that the creative content had to be relevant, simple, memorable, honest and believable…
"If it didn't sell, it wasn't creative."
Jacobson Advertising quickly grew into one of Seattle's largest creative retail advertising agencies.

Today, the concept of "branding" has replaced what we once referred to as "corporate identity". In a few years, just about everyone will have a cell phone/computer and access to all the world's products and services. Drone delivery to specific locations may become commonplace. These devices will have a more powerful reach than any other medium has ever had and targeting them will be absolutely necessary for every business.

Now is the time for simple, relevant, memorable creative communication—it has never been more important! To compete, advertisers must have short, distinctive, memorable and relative names, slogans and logos. They must have unique selling propositions that can be quickly demonstrated (and believed) to maximize their potential.

The Ones - The Loved Ones - The Crazy Ones

Here's to <u>the loved ones</u>.
Those individuals who are always there,
even though it may be years since the last time you last
saw them. <u>The ones</u> in your life who are always there.
<u>The ones</u> who want you in their lives
and will do anything to make you smile.
<u>The ones </u>who love you no matter what.

Here's to <u>the crazy ones</u>.
The misfits. The rebels. The troublemakers.
The round pegs in square holes.
<u>The ones</u> who see things differently.
They're not fond of rules,
and they have no respect for the status quo.
They question everything.
They push the human race forward.
And while some may see them as <u>the crazy ones</u>,
I see them as geniuses.
Because the people who are crazy enough
to think they can change the world, are <u>the ones</u> who can.

The coming and going numbers...

111,111,111, x 111,111,111, = 12,345,678,987,654,321

In this small book,
1,111 HIP-POCKET APHORISMS—
wit and ideas become
an unlimited resource for fertile minds
with imagination, independence, tolerance,
aloneness, effective communication, joyfulness,
optimism, and dynamism—
wit and ideas all related to creativity and self-sufficiency.

Now that you are aware of the number 111,
you will see <u>the ones</u> all around you.

CRAB-BAIT.COM

I illustrated the CRAB BAIT & HAIRBALL aphorisms cartoon concept in 2002. I then shelved the project as a number of other ventures had fluttered into my butterfly mind.

Now, in the twilight of mediocre career, I have combined the CRAB BAIT & HAIRBALL cartoons with personal selections from my collection of over 1,000 creative aphorisms into this book…

CRAB BAIT

Family isn't always blood. It's people in your life who want you in theirs. <u>The ones</u> who would do anything to see you smile, and love you no matter what.

& HAIRBALL

1,111

HIP-POCKET APHORISMS
Ken Jacobson

IF YOU STEAL FROM ONE IT IS PLAGIARISM... IF YOU STEAL FROM MANY, IT'S RESEARCH... THIS BOOK IS WELL-RESEARCHED.

Cartoons by Ken Jacobson

CRAB BAIT & HAIRBALL 1,111 HIP-POCKET APHORISMS

PLATYPUS CREATIVE

A private publisher

$11.11 ea. @ crab-bait.com
Also available thru Amazon.com

LIBRARY OF CONGRESS CATALOGING-IN-PUBLICATION DATA

Jacobson, Ken, 1938–

CRAB BAIT & HAIRBALL 1,111 HIP-POCKET APHORISMS

ISBN-13: 9781730717079 (CreateSpace)
APHORISMS / WISDOM / SAYINGS / HUMOR / METAPHOR / PUNS
TRUISMS / QUOTES / QUOTATIONS / PROVERB / ADAGE / AXIOMS
LEXOPHILIA / PARADOXES / PARAPROSDOKIANS / BRITTANYS

TABLE OF CONTENTS

Legend –

CB – "CRAB BAIT"
HB – "HAIRBALL"
MO – "MO"
D – "DIRT"

CRAB BAIT, HAIRBALL, MO & DIRT are a dog, a cat, a mouse and a rat living with an urban family to whom they refer to dutifully and collectively as "BOSS". BOSS thinks CRAB BAIT and HAIRBALL are their pets, but the four roomies know that the opposite is true… they all own BOSS' family.

CRAB BAIT is a Brittany, a pointing bird dog. His dad is a Hall of Fame National Dual Champion. He is an observant, intellectual philosopher with a very dry wit and likes to show it off with sage comments and explanations of aphorisms, sayings, one-liners, etc. He was named as a pup when BOSS said if he didn't hunt…"He will become CRAB BAIT". He is, however, because of his breeding, a great little bird dog when he goes hunting…but mostly he takes BOSS for walks.

One of his house mates (not by choice) is a long-hair cat called HAIRBALL, a neutered male cat that is a self-centered hyper-active (when he is awake) introvert that walks around on the tips of his claws. HAIRBALL is dumb. Occasionally, however, brilliance erupts, mostly by accident. He takes care of himself, leaving a con-trail

1

or nest of hair wherever he goes. He sleeps constantly, except at feeding time or high-activity periods, which occasionally occur when he decides he is going to do something…his way. HAIRBALL'S name is very descriptive, just nudging out HAIRBRAIN.

CRAB BAIT & HAIRBALL demand food, shelter and attention when they want it. CRAB BAITS' responsibility is to bark at intruders, delivery men and visitors. He is also expected to take BOSS on walks and point and retrieve birds, should BOSS go bird hunting and get lucky shooting.

MO, a house mouse, is CRAB BAIT'S best friend. MO is much brighter than and likes to play mind games with HAIRBALL and DIRT. Mo also likes to make DIRT the straight man and put the blame on him.

DIRT is a rat. He is always a couple steps behind MO. He has attitude and inadequacy problems, thinks he is constantly belittled and has received a bad rap because everyone keeps referring to him as a "dirty rat".

The foursome has made a pact to work together, are good friends, and consider themselves part of the BOSS family. MO has orchestrated a plan to make CRAB BAIT and HAIRBALL look good by conducting occasional "chases" and "catches" of both MO and DIRT. It is all for show, causing BOSS to make comments like "Good Hunter" and "Great Mouser". The plan guarantees room and board for the foursome.

CRAB BAIT & HAIRBALL
HIP-POCKET APHORISMS:

An aphorism (pronounced *AFF-or-ism*) is a short memorable statement. These pearls of condensed wisdom can "jump out" and provide instant solutions, direction and understanding. Simplified aphorisms, sayings or one-liners can quickly recognize complex situations and determine a solution. They are easy to remember sayings, truisms or statements of communication. They can be statements of truth or opinions expressed in short, concise and witty manners. They can just be fun reading.

Wordsmiths have definitions and explanations of creative communication that separately identify a concept differently from what I am generally calling "aphorisms". The list includes: proverbs / adages / truisms / metaphors

/ quotes / axioms / puns / oxymorons / paradoxes / paraprosdokians / lexophilia, etc.

CRAB BAIT & HAIRBALL aphorisms are from my collection over the past fifty years of a hip-pocket creativity, memorable observations, witty one-liners, short-sayings of good advice, general truths and insights that can apply to a variety of situations, as well as, just be plain entertaining to read. **(Hip-pocket is a metaphor for a personal place to keep your valuable earnings and learning.)** It also appears that short-sayings helped grow America as it was settled by explorers, ranchers and farmers whose focus was on work and not words. The wisdom of American Indians was sage and profound, but mostly ignored by mainstream publications.

<u>A good aphorism can really stick in the mind.</u> Because they're short, aphorisms are easy to remember, and they often employ striking metaphors that give them even more staying power. The best aphorisms are also applicable to all sorts of different situations, which further ads to their memorable quality. People who write good aphorisms are seen as extremely wise, and their words have the power to inspire us even (in some cases) a thousand years after the writer has died.

What you gain with aphorisms is staying power and general applicability. What you lose sometimes is clarity and specificity. Precisely because they're so short, aphorisms don't leave room for supporting arguments or clarification. There's always the risk that readers will misunderstand what you mean to say. You also leave yourself open to the charge that what you're writing is not an aphorism but a truism, (or some other word form) which essentially means that the aphorism lacks real meaning or significance. I view aphorisms as creative communications. *It takes a narrow mind to only be able to spell a word one way.*

Proverb/Adage –

Most proverbs are aphorisms, but they don't originate with a specific author. Whereas aphorisms sometimes have a single author who invented them, proverbs generally don't – they just emerge from folk wisdom or the general culture. (Scriptures sometimes use the word somewhat differently, for example in "The Proverbs of Solomon," which may or may not have had a single author.) The words "proverb" and "adage" are synonymous.

Truism –

A truism is an aphorism that is trite, stale, overly general, or meaningless. It's an aphorism that is so obviously true that it lacks any significance. People disagree about which aphorisms are truisms, but one common example is "the journey of a thousand miles begins with a single step" (Lao Zi). Some people find this aphorism to be profound and inspiring, but others would say that it's obvious and brings no new information—then it's a truism.

Metaphor –

The primary tool of many aphorisms is **metaphor**, or having one thing stand in for something else. Take, for example, the aphorism - "If the shoe fits, wear it." In this case, "shoe" is a metaphor for all sorts of things—jobs, partners, opportunities, or anything else that might "fit" in a general sense. Of course, there are some aphorisms that are simple statements of truth without any metaphors.

Quote/Quotation –

A quote or **quotation** is any excerpt of another person's speech or writing. The most popular quotations are generally aphorisms, because they're short and concise, and therefore easy to remember and share. (Most people use the words "quote" and "quotation" interchangeably, but strict grammarians will insist that "quote" is a verb, while "quotation" is the noun.)

Axiom –

An **axiom** or postulate is a statement that is taken to be true, to serve as a premise or starting point for further reasoning and arguments. The word comes from the Greek axíōma, that which is thought worthy or fit' or 'that which commends itself as evident.' The term has subtle differences in definition when used in the context of different fields of study. As defined in classic philosophy, an axiom is a statement that is so evident or well-established, that it is accepted...

Lexophilia –

Lexophilia is the love of words. The term, a neologism and unofficial word of the English language, derives from two Greek words—lexis, a derivative of the Greek logos meaning "word," and philia, meaning "friendship" or "fondness."

Paraprosdokian –

A **paraprosdokian** is a figure of speech in which the latter part of a sentence, phrase, or larger discourse is surprising or unexpected in a way that causes the reader or listener to reframe or reinterpret the first part. It is frequently used for humorous or dramatic effect, sometimes producing an anticlimax. For this reason, it is extremely popular among comedians and satirists.

Pun –

A **pun** is a play on words, either on different senses of the same word or on the similar sense or sound of different words. Known in rhetoric as paronomasia. **Puns** are figures of speech based on the inherent ambiguities of language. Although **puns** are commonly regarded as a childish form of humor, they are often found in advertisements and newspaper headlines.

Oxymoron –

A figure of speech in which two opposite ideas are joined to create an effect. The common oxymoron phrase is a combination of an adjective proceeded by a noun with contrasting meanings, such as "cruel kindness," or "living death". The contrasting words/phrases are not always glued together. The contrasting ideas may be spaced out in a sentence, such as, "In order to lead, you must walk behind."

Confucius –

Confucius was a Chinese teacher, editor, politician, and philosopher of the Spring and Autumn period of Chinese history. The philosophy of Confucius, also known as Confucianism, emphasized personal and governmental morality, correctness of social relationships, justice and sincerity. His followers competed successfully with many other schools during the Hundred Schools of Thought era only to be suppressed in favor of the Legalists during the Qin Dynasty.

8

APHORISM:

"A short, pointed sentence
that expresses a wise or clever
observation or a general truth."

CRAB-BAIT.com

<u>Political Aphorisms</u>

If God wanted us to vote,
he would have given us candidates.
~Jay Leno~

When I was a boy I was told that anybody could become
President; I'm beginning to believe it.
~Clarence Darrow~

The problem with political jokes is they get elected.
~Henry Cate, VII~

We hang the petty thieves and appoint the great ones to
public office.
~Aesop~

If we got one-tenth of what was promised to us in these
State of the Union speeches, there wouldn't be any
inducement to go to heaven.
~Will Rogers~

Politicians are the same all over. They promise to build a
bridge even where there is no river.
~Nikita Khrushchev~

Why pay money to have your family tree traced; go into
politics and your opponents will do it for you.
~Author unknown~

Politicians are people who, when they see light at the end
of the tunnel, go out and buy some more tunnel.
~John Quinton~

Politics is the gentle art of getting votes from the poor
and campaign funds from the rich, by promising to
protect each from the other.
~Oscar Ameringer~
(I particularly like this last one!)

I offer my opponents a bargain: if they will stop telling
lies about us, I will stop telling the truth about them.
~Adlai Stevenson, campaign speech, 1952~

A politician is a fellow who will lay down
your life for his country.
~Tex Guinan~

I have come to the conclusion that politics is too serious a
matter to be left to the politicians.
~Charles de Gaulle~

Instead of giving a politician the keys to the city, it might
be better to change the locks.
~Doug Larson~

If you want a real friend that you can trust
in Washington get a dog.
~Harry Truman~
(I like the way Harry thinks!)

We have the best government money can buy.
~Mark Twain~

Politicians and diapers need to be changed regularly,
usually for the same reasons.
~Anonymous~

"Politics: 'Poli', a Latin word meaning 'many', and
'tics', meaning 'bloodsucking creatures'."
~Robin Williams~

Pay for everything out of your
HIP-POCKET NATIONAL BANK.
"To double your money. Fold it…
Then put it in your hip-pocket."

"Twenty years from now you will be more disappointed by the things that you didn't do than by the ones you did do.
So throw off the bowlines.
Sail away from the safe harbor.
Catch the trade winds in your sails…"

EXPLORE! DREAM! DISCOVER!
–Mark Twain

"I've boiled my life down to <u>my family</u>, <u>my friends</u>, <u>my memories</u> and <u>my dreams</u>."
–Ken Jacobson

"God is a Verb."

"I live in my children and my children's children."

"A man with a gun can rob a bank.
A bank can rob everyone."

"To hunt is <u>to live</u>, <u>to learn</u>, <u>to remember</u> and <u>to dream</u>."

"I'd rather have it, than have it to get."

"If they are talking about me,
then you are leaving someone else alone."

"Records live... Opinions die."

"Tact is the ability to tell someone to go to hell in such a
way that they look forward to the trip."

"It's all about money."

"Time crumbles everything."

"We are what we repeatedly do."

"Success is the ability to go from one failure to another
without the loss of enthusiasm."

"Class requires style... But style doesn't make class."

"Living causes dying."

When you were born, you cried and the world rejoiced.
Live your life so that when you die,
the world cries and you rejoice.
Cherokee

"Anything worth dying for is certainly worth living for."

"Man loves company…
even if it is only that of a small burning candle."

"Replace the "W" with a "T"
and you have the answer to
What, Where, and When?

"Be true to yourself."

"Make teachers of both your friends and enemies."

"The best way to tell a lie is to tell 99% of the truth."

"Great minds discuss ideas;
Average minds discuss events;
Small minds discuss people."

"Always keep you enemies in front of you."

"Always chase rainbows!"

"Rainbow is my favorite color."

"Handy as an extra pocket on a shirt."

"Retired… everyday is Saturday."

"There is only one place to bury a loved one…
That's in your heart!"

"All great words of wisdom
can be reduced to a T-shirt slogan,
(or a bumper sticker, if you are really good.)"

"I think women are foolish to pretend they are equal to men; they are far superior and always have been.

"Whatever you give a woman, she will make it greater. If you give her sperm, she'll give you a baby. If you give her a house, she'll give you a home. If you give her groceries, she'll give you a meal. If you give her a smile, she'll give you her heart. She multiplies and enlarges whatever is given to her. So… if you give her any crap— be ready to get a ton of it!!"

"A wise man once said nothing"

"If a woman says 'first of all' during an argument,
run away. Because she has prepared
research, data, charts and will destroy you."

"Some things are just better left unsaid.
And I usually realize it right after I say them."

Every time you talk to your wife,
your mind should remember that…
*"This conversation will be recorded for training and
quality purposes."*

"Behind every angry woman, stands a man who has
absolutely no idea what he did wrong."

"When a woman is talking to you,
listen to what she says with her eyes."

"Never make a woman mad. They can remember stuff
that hasn't even happened yet."

"Forgive your enemies – It messes with their heads."

"I don't need anger management.
I need people to stop pissing me off."

"Be the kind of person you pet thinks you are."

"The biggest lie I tell myself is…
I don't need to write that down, I'll remember it."

"Even duct tape can't fix stupid,
but it can muffle the sound."

Getting "lucky" means walking into a room and
remembering why you're there.

"Yes, officer, I did see the 'Speed Limit Sign',
I just didn't see you."

"Sometimes just getting out of bed ruins the whole day."

"How can eating a two-pound box of chocolates make
me gain five pounds?"

"I have learned that to ignore the facts, does not change
the facts."

"Laws are silent in times of war."

"When eagles are silent… parrots begin to jabber."

Coyote is always out there waiting,
and Coyote is always hungry.
Navajo

"In everything...
That which is least expected is most esteemed."

"If you don't stand for something,
you will fall for everything."

"Anger is an acid that can do more to the vessel in which
it is stored than anything on which it is poured."

"You can't beat a colt for being a colt."

"Happiness, Health, Laughter and Joy
follow a smiling face."

"A smile is a language that even a baby understands."

"Life isn't tied with a bow, but it's still a gift."

The simplest words..."yes" and "no"...
take the most thought

One tequila, two tequila, three tequila......Floor.

"He is a self-made man and worships his Creator."
–*John Bright*

Atheism is a non-prophet organization.

If man evolved from monkeys and apes,
why do we still have monkeys and apes?

I went to a bookstore and asked the saleswoman,
"Where's the self-help section?"
She said if she told me, it would defeat the purpose.

Just as the graveside service finished, there was a distant
lightning bolt accompanied by a tremendous burst of
rumbling thunder. The little man looked at the Pastor and
calmly said, "Well, she's there and
it's His problem now."

What if there were no hypothetical questions?

If a deaf child signs swear words,
does his mother wash his hands with soap?

If someone with multiple personalities threatens to kill
himself, is it considered a hostage situation?

Is there another word for synonym?

Where do forest rangers go to "get away from it all?"

Each bird loves to hear himself sing.
Arapaho

What do you do when you see an endangered animal
eating an endangered plant?

If a parsley farmer is sued, can they garnish his wages?

Would a fly without wings be called a walk?

Why do they lock gas station bathrooms?
Are they afraid someone will break in and clean them?

If a turtle doesn't have a shell,
is it homeless or naked?

Can vegetarians eat animal crackers?

If the police arrest a mute, do they tell him he has the right to remain silent?

Why do they put braille
on the drive-through bank machines?

How do they get deer to cross the road only at those yellow road signs?

What was the best thing before sliced bread?

One nice thing about egotists:
they don't talk about other people.

Does the little mermaid wear an algebra?
(*This one took me a minute*)

Do infants enjoy infancy
as much as adults enjoy adultery?

How is it possible to have a civil war?

If one synchronized swimmer drowns,
do the rest drown too?

It's all about money!

"Chase Rainbows."

"My favorite color is rainbow!"

"Every man is a hero to his own imagination."

"Nature does nothing needlessly."

"The longer you live...
the less importance you apply to importance."

"We are known by the friends we keep."

"Assume you're wrong... Then prove you're right."

"For a moment...A lie is the truth."

"There is only one chance
to make a first or last impression."

"Speak softly and carry a big stick."

"The easiest way to eat crow is when it's warm.
The colder it gets, the harder it is to swallow."

"Being a good citizen means being able and
ready to pull you own weight."

"Success is the size a hole a man leaves after he dies."

"If I had a dollar for every girl that found me
unattractive, they'd eventually find me attractive."

"I find it ironic that the colors red, white, and blue stand
for freedom, until they're flashing behind you."

"Today a man knocked on my door and asked for a small
donation towards the local swimming pool,
so I gave him a glass of water."

"Artificial intelligence is no match for natural stupidity."

"I'm great at multi-tasking—I can waste time,
be unproductive, and procrastinate all at once."

"If you can smile when things go wrong,
you have someone in mind to blame."

"Take my advice—I'm not using it."

"Hospitality is the art of making guests feel like they're at home when you wish they were."

"Behind every great man is a woman rolling her eyes."

"Ever stop to think and forget to start again?"

"Women spend more time wondering what men are thinking than men spend thinking."

"Is it wrong that only one company makes the game Monopoly?"

"Women sometimes make fools of men, but most guys are the do-it-yourself type."

"I was going to give him a nasty look, but he already had one."

"I was going to wear my camouflage shirt today, but I couldn't find it."

"Sometimes I wake up grumpy; other times I let her sleep."

"If tomatoes are technically a fruit, is ketchup a smoothie?"

"Money is the root of all wealth."

"No matter how much you push the envelope, it'll still be stationery."

"Music is what feelings sound like."

"Yesterday is a cashed check."

"Man is the only animal that blushes, or needs to."

"Do what you can, with what you have, where you are."

"Never ask a barber if you need a haircut."

"Brains in the head save blisters on the feet."

There is nothing as eloquent as a rattlesnake's tail.
Navajo

"Thunder is impressive...
But it's lightning that does the job."

"The reward of a thing done well is to have done it."

"Our time on earth is our heaven."

What is life? It is the flash of a firefly in the night. It is
the breath of a buffalo in the wintertime. It is the little
shadow which runs across the grass
and loses itself in the sunset.
Blackfoot

"Choose a job you love,
and you will never work a day in your life."

"The thing you need most is the thing you need
when you need it."

"Never play a man at his own game."

"If you are the fastest gun...
Remember there is always someone faster."

"Nothing great was ever achieved without enthusiasm."

"It doesn't matter which road you're taking,
if you don't know where you're going."

Good bird dogs are not for sale.

Good horses are not for sale.

"There is only one place to bury your best friend...
that's in your heart."

"What is moral is what you feel good after..."

"Load your brain before you shoot off your mouth."

"It's all about money."

"Nothing really exists, everything that is, was."

"All life is an experiment."

If you ate both pasta and antipasto,
would you still be hungry?

If you try to fail, and succeed, which have you done?

Whose cruel idea was it for the word 'lisp'
to have 's' in it?

Why are hemorrhoids called "hemorrhoids"
instead of "assteroids?"

Why is it called tourist season if we can't shoot at them?

Why is there an expiration date on sour cream?

If you spin an oriental man in a circle three times,
does he become disoriented?

Can an atheist get insurance against acts of god?

Why do shops have signs, "guide dogs only?"
The dogs can't read, and their owners are blind.

Don't do drugs.
I find I get the same effect just by standing up really fast.

I don't like political jokes.
I've seen too many get elected.

The most precious thing we have is life,
yet it has absolutely no trade-in value.

"Nothing is stronger than habit."

Every day I beat my previous record of consecutive days
I've stayed alive.

Eventually, people will realize that mistakes
are meant for learning, not repeating.

No one ever says, "it's only a game!"
when their team's winning.

Ever notice that people who spend money on beer,
cigarettes and lottery tickets are always complaining
about being broke and not feeling well?

Isn't having a smoking section in a restaurant like having
a peeing section in a swimming pool?

Marriage changes passion…
Suddenly you're in bed with a relative.

Now that food has replaced sex in my life,
I can't even get into my own pants.

I signed up for an exercise class and was told to wear
loose-fitting clothing. If I had any loose-fitting clothing,
I wouldn't need the freakin' class!

Don't argue with an idiot; people watching may not be
able to tell the difference.

Wouldn't you know it! Brain cells come,
and brain cells go, but fat cells live forever.

Beware of those who would ask you to sacrifice…for
they would make you the slave and themselves master.

"It's not the biggest, swiftness or smartest,
that wins the race...
But it is the way to bet."

"There is as much dignity in plowing a field,
as there is in writing a poem."

"The secret to a secret
is to know when and how to tell it."

"Life's tough, the first hundred years are the hardest."

"Innovate, never pioneer...
There are too many pioneers with arrows in their backs."

"The more I learn, the less I know."

"We only get one chance
to dance the first and last dance."

"There are two sides to every pancake."

"You cannot teach a crab to walk straight."

"Only a fool argues with a skunk, a mule or a cook."

"We plant trees for the benefit of another generation."

"My photographs don't do me justice—
they look just like me."

"I asked the waiter, "Is this milk fresh?" He said,
"Three hours ago it was grass."

"The reason the golf pro tells you to keep your head
down is so you can't see him laughing."

"Money will buy a fine dog,
but only kindness will make him wag his tail."

"Tranquilizers work only if you follow the advice
on the bottle—Keep away from children."

"You know you are old if they have discontinued
your blood type."

"Trust your heart, but do nothing in a heat of passion."

Don't be afraid to cry.
It will free your mind of sorrowful thoughts.
Hopi

"When people talk, listen. Most people never listen."

"It is really simple.
If you say you're going to do something, do it!
If you start something, finish it!"

"History is the version of past events
that people have decided to agree upon."
–*Napoleon*

"Questions are always more important than words."

"To find truth, love truth and despise truths."

"Youth is totally experimental."

"If you don't have a sense of humor, you probably don't
have any sense at all.

"Stroke a cat, and you have a permanent job."

"No one has a more driving ambition that a teenage boy
who wants to buy a car."

"There are worse things than getting a call for a wrong
number at 4 am; for example, it could be the right
number."

"Be careful about reading the fine print, there's no way
you're going to like it.

"Money can't buy happiness, but somehow it's more
comfortable to cry in a Jaguar than in a Ford."

Day and night cannot dwell together.
Duwamish

"White man builds a big fire then stands way back...
Indian builds a small fire then gets up close."

We will be known forever by the tracks we leave.
Dakota

"Question everything!"

"Live as if you were to die tomorrow.
Learn as if you were to live forever."

"Don't wait for flowers, plant your own garden".

"If you tell the truth,
you don't have anything to remember."

"No one can make you feel inferior
without your consent."

"Kenny Ray, what did Lecil say?"

"Language is the source of misunderstandings."

"The eyes are blind…one must see with the heart."

"A butterfly is the caterpillar's end of the world."

"Not all who wander are lost."

"It don't take a genius to spot a goat in a flock of sheep."

"Sometimes you get and sometimes you get got."

"Telling a man to get lost and making him do it
are two different propositions."

"If you attempt to rob a bank you won't have any trouble
with rent/food for the next 10 years,
whether or not you are successful."

"Do twins ever realize that one of them is unplanned?"

"What if my dog only brings back my ball because he
thinks I like throwing it?"

"If poison expires,
is it more poisonous or is it no longer poisonous?"

"Which letter is silent in the word "Scent,"
the S or the C?"

"The letter W, in English, is called double U.
Shouldn't it be called double V?"

"Maybe oxygen is slowly killing you and it just takes
75–100 years to fully work."

"Every time you clean something,
you just make something else dirty."

"The word 'swims' upside-down is still 'swims'."

"100 years ago everyone owned a horse and only the rich
had cars. Today everyone has cars
and only the rich own horses."

"Your future self is watching you right now
through memories."

"If you're riding ahead of the herd, take a look back
every now and then to make sure they are with ya."

"Always take a look at what you're about to eat.
It's not so important to know what it is,
but it's crucial to know what it was."

"The quickest way to double your money is to fold it
and put it in your pocket."

"You're as handy as an extra pocket in a shirt."

"A man will stand on his brother's head
if he's drowning."

"Talk low, talk slow and don't say too much."

"Courage is being scared to death
and saddling up anyway."

Whatever you do in life, do the very best you can with
both your heart and your mind.
Lakota Sioux

"Life is simpler when you plow around a stump."

"Words that soak into your ears are whispered…
not yelled."

No matter where you go… there you are."

"Meanness don't just happen overnight."

"Don't cry because it's over…
smile because it happened."

"Do not corner something that is meaner than you."

"Everyone lies, but it doesn't matter,
because no one listens."

"You cannot unsay a cruel word."

"It doesn't take a big person to carry a grudge."

"Most of the stuff people worry about,
ain't never gonna happen anyway."

"Life is not always fair.
Sometimes you get a splinter sliding down a rainbow."

"If you get to thinking you're a person of some influence,
try ordering somebody else's dog around."

"Don't pick a fight with an old man.
If he is too old to fight, he'll just kill you."

"Good judgment comes from experience,
and a lot of that comes from bad judgment."

"Never miss a good chance to shut up."

"People are prisoners of their cell phones."

"Better to remain silent and be assumed a fool,
than to speak and remove all doubt."

"When you lose, don't lose the lesson."

"Age is an issue of mind over matter.
If you don't mind, it doesn't matter."

"Don't interfere with something
that ain't bothering you none."

"Today is my favorite day!"

"Moral indignation is jealousy with a halo."

"Silence is golden when you can't think of
a good answer."

"Law, by definition,
cannot obey the same rules as nature."

"Accept the past as the past,
without denying it or discarding it."

"Life, if well-lived, is long enough."

Pigs get fat; hogs get slaughtered.

A worm is the only animal that can't fall down.

Just because a chicken has wings don't mean it can fly.

Keep your saddle oiled and your gun greased.

You can't get lard unless you boil the hog.

If you cut your own firewood, it'll warm you twice.

Give me the bacon without the sizzle.

Don't hang your wash on someone else's line.

A guilty fox hunts his own hole.

Be someone who makes you happy.

The barn door's open and the mule's trying to run.
(Your fly's down.)

Don't squat on your spurs.

Any mule's tail can catch cockleburs.

A drought usually ends with a flood.

If you lie down with dogs, you get up with fleas.

No, we do not have Wi-Fi… talk to each other.

Life is sexually transmitted.

Don't worry about old age… It doesn't last that long.

When you die, you will be spoken of
as those in the sky, like the stars.
Yurok

I'll wear my Sunday-go-to-meeting clothes.

He's all gussied up.

Fat as a boardinghouse cat.

A cactus is just a really aggressive cucumber.

He don't care what you call him,
as long as you call him to supper.

Don't make me UPPER CASE!

One man with conviction will overwhelm
a hundred who only have opinions.

Tetris is life.
Mistakes pile up and achievements disappear.

He's big enough to bear-hunt with a switch.

Wide as two axe handles.

He'll eat anything that don't eat him first.

A beauty parlor is a place where women
curl up and dye.

Tight as a tick.

Tight as a fiddle string.

Seek wisdom, not knowledge. Knowledge is of the past.
Wisdom is of the future.
Lumbee

Chickens are the only animals you eat
before they are born *and* after they die.

Tight as a wet boot.

Tight enough to raise a blister.

He'll squeeze a nickel till the buffalo screams.

He has short arms and deep pockets.

He's got a big hole in his screen door.

He's one bubble off plumb.

He's two sandwiches short of a picnic.

He's a few pickles short of a barrel.

He's missing a few buttons off his shirt.

A committee is a body that
keeps minutes and wastes hours.

He's overdrawn at the memory bank.

I hear you clucking, but I can't find your nest.

A cup of water is just a domesticated puddle.

Dust is mud with its juice squeezed out.

They tried to hang him, but the rope broke.

He could draw a pat hand from a stacked deck.

He always draws the best bull.

He's riding a gravy train with biscuit wheels.

He could sit on the fence and the birds would feed him.

An egotist is someone who is usually
me-deep in conversation.

If a man is to do something more than human, he must
have more than human powers.
Tribe Unknown

A handkerchief is cold storage.

So rich they can eat fried chicken all week long.

Rich enough to eat her laying hens.

If a trip around the world cost a dollar,
I couldn't get to the state line.

Hasn't got a pot to pee in or a window to throw it out of.

The bird that has eaten
cannot fly with bird that is hungry.
Omaha

Regard Heaven as your Father, Earth as your Mother and
all things as your Brothers and Sisters.
Tribe Unknown

I ate so many armadillos when I was young,
I still roll up into a ball when I hear a dog bark.

A mosquito is an insect that makes you like flies better.

Your skull doesn't have a facial expression.
Your flesh just moves around.

He's broke as a stick horse.

He's too poor to pay attention.

Inflation is cutting money in half
without damaging the paper.

So poor their Sunday supper is fried water.

Too poor to paint, too proud to whitewash.

Hot as Hades.

A raisin is a grape with a sunburn.

Hot as a depot stove.

Hot as a two-dollar pistol.

A secret is something you tell to one person at a time.

Hot as a billy goat in a pepper patch.

A skeleton is a bunch of bones with the body scraped off.

Hot enough to fry eggs on the sidewalk.

Toothache is the pain that drives you to extraction.

Hotter than a honeymoon hotel.

Hotter than a preacher's knee.

Hotter than a burning stump.

Hotter than blue blazes.

So hot the hens are laying hard-boiled eggs.

Cold as an ex-wife's heart.

Cold as a cast-iron commode.

Cold as a banker's heart.

"Diplomacy is the art of saying 'Nice doggie,'
until you can find a rock."
–Will Rogers

A yawn is an honest opinion openly expressed.

"I remain just one thing,
and one thing only, and that is a clown.
It places me on a far higher plane than any politician."
–Charlie Chaplin

A good chief gives, he does not take.
Mohawk

Tomorrow is one of the greatest labor-saving
devices of today.

A people without a history are like
the wind over buffalo grass.
Sioux

You look like you were sent for and couldn't go.

Sad enough to bring a tear to a glass eye.

He looks like the cheese fell off his cracker.

She wears her bra backwards and it fits.

He's knee-high to a grasshopper.

He'd have to stand up to look a rattler in the eye.

About as big as the little end of nothing.

Half as big as a minute.

44

It is less of a problem to be poor,
than it is to be dishonest.
Anishinabe

Wrinkles are something other people have,
similar to my character lines.

Nothing between the horns and hooves but hide.

Is it good if a vacuum really sucks?

Thin as a gnat's whisker.

Thin as store-bought thread.

Thin as Depression soup.

Thin as a rake and twice as sexy.

Flat as a fritter.

Why is the third hand on a watch called the second hand?

If a word is misspelled in the dictionary,
how would we ever know?

So skinny she has to stand twice to make a shadow.

So skinny she shades herself under the clothesline.

If Webster wrote the first dictionary,
where did he find the words?

Don't let yesterday use up too much of today.
Cherokee

Cheese is just a loaf of milk.

He was born sorry

He's so low he'd steal the widow's ax.

He'd steal his mama's egg money.

He'd steal the flowers off his grandma's grave.

He'd steal the nickels off a dead man's eyes.

No-account fellow.

Why do we say something is out of whack?
What is a whack?

Tough as nickel steak.

Mean as a mama wasp.

Why do "slow down" and "slow up"
mean the same thing?

She makes a hornet look cuddly.

Why do "fat chance" and "slim chance"
mean the same thing?

Rough as a cob.

Listening to a liar is like drinking warm water.
Tribe Unknown

Sign at a church: Adultery is a sin.
You can't have your Kate and Edith too.

He's got horns holding up his halo.

Why do "tug boats" push their barges?

He's so low you couldn't put a rug under him.

He jumped on me with all four feet.

Why do we sing "Take me out to the ball game"
when we are already there?

He jumped on me like a duck on a June bug.

He jumped on me like white on rice.

When a fox walks lame, the old rabbit jumps.
Oklahoma

He can blow out the lamp and jump into bed
before it gets dark.

Why are they called "stands"
when they are made for sitting?

Quick out of the chute.

Fast as greased lightning.

Fast as small-town gossip.

Faster than a prairie fire with a tail wind.

Faster than a scalded cat.

Faster than double-struck lightning.

Faster than a sneeze through a screen door.

Going like a house afire.

Hell-bent for leather.

Any faster and he'd catch up to yesterday.

B1... The vitamin for making friends.

Why is it called "after dark"
when it is really "after light"?

His breath's so strong
you could hang out the washing on it.

That coffee's so strong it'll put hair on your chest.

Coffee so strong it'll walk into your cup.

He's so strong he makes Samson look sensitive.

Look what the cat dragged in.

Company's coming; add a cup of water to the soup.

Doesn't "expecting the unexpected" make the
unexpected expected?

If love is blind, why is lingerie so popular?

It's time to heat up the bricks.

Everyone who is successful
must have dreamed of something.
Maricopa

I worked most of my life to become an overnight success.

It's time to put the chairs in the wagon.

It's time to swap spit and hit the road.

It's time to put out the fire and call in the dogs.

Let's blow this pop stand.

Why are a "wise man" and a "wise guy" opposites?

How come abbreviated is such a long word?

Why is "phonics" not spelled the way it sounds?

Take a tater and wait.

Don't get your panties in a wad.

Looks like she was rode hard and put away wet.

He looks like Bowser's bone.

I was born tired and I've since suffered a relapse.

One wheel down and the axle dragging.

Why do "overlook" and "oversee" mean opposite things?

One rain does not make a crop.
Creole

If work is so terrific,
why do they have to pay you to do it?

Why is bra singular and panties plural?

If the world is a stage, where is the audience sitting?

Old ways won't open new doors.

I'm so sick I'd have to get better to die.

Why do we wash bath towels?
Aren't we clean after we use them?

You never achieve success
unless you like what you are doing.

Successful people never worry
about what others are doing.

Why do you press harder on the buttons of a remote
control when you know the batteries are dead?

As full of pains as an old window.

I've got the green apple nasties.

He looks like death warmed over.

So sick he needs two beds.

Why do we put suits in garment bags
and garments in suitcases?

She could talk a coon right out of a tree.

He could talk the legs off a chair.

He could talk the gate off its hinges.

He could talk the hide off a cow.

He could talk the ears off a mule.

He shoots off his mouth so much
he must eat bullets for breakfast.

He's got a ten-gallon mouth.

She speaks ten words a second, with gusts to fifty.

Her tongue is plumb tuckered.

She's got tongue enough for ten rows of teeth.

She beats her own gums to death.

Christmas is the time of year that we sit in front of dead trees and eat candy out of socks.

Why do they call it a TV set when you only have one?

He was vaccinated with a Victrola needle.

Nervous as a whore in church.

Grinning like a mule eating cockleburs.

Nervous as a pregnant jenny.

Nervous as a fly in the glue pot.

Nervous as a woodshed waiter.

Don't dig up more snakes than you can kill.

Whistle before you walk into a stranger's camp.

Don't plow too close to the cotton.

A dead snake can still bite.

A dead bee can still sting.

Don't tip over the outhouse.

Even a blind hog can find an acorn once in a while.

Anytime you happen to pass my house,
I'd sure appreciate it.

What did you do with the money your mama gave you
for singing lessons?

Were you raised in a barn?

Put that in your pipe and smoke it.

Even the chickens under the porch know that.

Man's law changes with his understanding of man. Only
the laws of the spirit remain always the same.
Crow

You smell like you want to be left alone.

Go peddle your own produce.

If you break your leg, don't come running to me.

Whatever greases your wagon.

Got a big hole in the fence.

I got my ox in a ditch.

He loaded the wrong wagon.

They hung the wrong horse thief.

He ripped his britches.

There's a yellowjacket in the outhouse.

Preaching to the choir.

Burning daylight.

Arguing with a wooden Indian.

He broke his arm patting himself on the back.

He thinks the sun comes up just to hear him crow.

I'd like to buy him for what he's worth
and sell him for what he thinks he'll bring.

She's so spoiled salt couldn't save her.

He wasn't born, just squeezed out of a bartender's rag.

Snot-slinging drunk.

Drunk as a fiddler's bitch.

Drunk as Cooter Brown.

Don't chop any wood tonight;
Daddy's coming home with a load.

In forty years, some of the recipes that we stole from
food blogs will be known as 'old family recipes'
by our grandchildren.

You can't wake a person who is pretending to be asleep.
Navajo

Drunk as a skunk.

Tighter than bark on a log.

I've got the whistle-belly thumps and skull cramps.
(A hangover.)

Calling for Earl or Ralph.
(Throwing up.)

Riding the porcelain pony.

Commode-hugging, knee-walking drunk.

Out where the buses don't run.

Buzzard bait.

He gave up his guitar for a harp.

He ate a bitter pill.

As welcome as an outhouse breeze.

As welcome as a porcupine at a nudist colony.

As welcome as a skunk at a lawn party.

As welcome as a wet shoe.

As welcome as a tornado on a trail drive.

No hill for a stepper.

Take care of your thoughts when you are alone…
Take care of your words when you are with people.

Beware of the man who does not talk,
and the dog that does not bark.
Cheyenne

Easy as pie.

Like trying to bag flies.

Like putting socks on a rooster.

Easy as pissing up a rope.

He blames everything on the weather or his raising.

He got caught in his own loop.

And God promised men that good and obedient wives
would be found in all corners of the world.
Then he made the Earth round...
and laughed and laughed and laughed...

Bright as a new penny.

Smart as a hooty owl.

No flies on my mama.

Smart as a whip.

If a duck had his brain, it would fly north for the winter.

She doesn't have enough sense to spit downwind.

If he was bacon, he wouldn't even sizzle.

If brains were leather, he couldn't saddle a flea.

He carries his brains in his back pocket.

Dumb as dirt.

Dumb as a box of rocks.

Dumb as a barrel of hair.

Dumb as a post.

Dumb as a wagon wheel.

Dumb as a prairie dog.

Dumb as a watermelon.

Dumb enough for twins.

He doesn't know "come here" from "sic-em."

He can't ride and chew at the same time.

So stupid, if you put his brains in a bumblebee,
it'd fly backwards.

If all her brains were dynamite,
she couldn't blow her nose.

If all her brains were ink, she couldn't dot an *i*.

He don't know which end's up.

He don't know a widget from a whang-doodle.

He don't know nothin' from nothing.

He don't know diddly-squat.

If he had a brain, it'd die of loneliness.

Don't pick the house flowers.

He couldn't pour piss out of a boot with a hole in the toe and the directions on the heel.

So thick-headed you can hit him in the face with a tire iron and he won't yell till morning.

He could screw up an anvil

He gave me the wire-brush treatment.

I got sandpapered.

I'll knock you plumb into next week.

When the smog lifts in Los Angeles, U.C.L.A.

He sure cleaned your plow.

Not what I had my face fixed for.

Like hugging a rose bush.

That dog won't hunt.

That dog will hunt.

I'd just as soon bite a bug.

I don't cotton to it.

Confused as a goat on Astro-Turf.

I can explain it to you. But I can't understand it for you.

He ran 'em around the barn.

The thief that stole a calendar got twelve months.

They call her "radio station" because anyone can pick her up, especially at night.

He's wilder than a peach orchard boar.

She's just naturally horizontal.

"Getting through life without a lot of
money, possessions, and/or friends
is admirable, especially if it is by choice."

"A reader lives a thousand lives before he dies."

"If you are not too long,
I will wait here for you all your life."

A man must make his own arrows.
Winnegago

"Your smile is your <u>logo</u>;
your personality is your <u>business card</u>;
how you leave others feeling after an experience
with you becomes your <u>trademark</u>."

"If the moon loves you, why worry about the stars?"

"Fake seems to be the latest trend
and everyone seems to be in style."

All of Creation is related, and the hurt of one is the hurt
of all. The honor of one is the honor of all. And whatever
we do affects everything in the Universe.
Lakota Sioux

63

Loose as ashes in the wind.

Loose as a bucket of soot.

Wilder than an acre of snakes.

She uses her sheet for a tablecloth.

He was born on the wrong side of the blanket.

She's found a new dasher for her churn.

They ate supper before they said grace.

They planted their crop before they built their fence.

They're hitched but not churched.

They've got a cotton-patch license.

She's got a bun in the oven.

She's sitting on the nest.

She's got one in the chute.

She's been storked.

Thousands of years ago, Cats were worshipped as Gods.
Cats have never forgotten that.

The batteries were given out free of charge.

Noisy as two skeletons dancing on a tin roof.

Noisy as a restless mule in a tin barn.

Noisier than cats making kittens.

Noisier than a cornhusk mattress.

Louder than Grandpa's Sunday tie.

He called his hogs all night.
(Snored.)

If you need a shoulder to cry on,
pull off to side of the road.

He could fall up a tree.

He couldn't knock a hole in the wind
with a sack full of hammers.

Couldn't ride a nightmare without falling out of bed.

So bad at farming he couldn't raise Cain.

He couldn't hit the floor if he fell out of bed.

Worthless as teats on a bull.

Not worth spit.

He couldn't organize a pissing contest in a brewery.

Useless as two buggies in a one-horse town.

He could screw up a two-car funeral.

Tie a quarter to it and throw it away.
Then you can say you lost something.

He's got no more chance than a June bug
in the chicken coop.

He's a day late and a dollar short.

He can't win for losing.

He's sucking hind teat.

To write with a broken pencil is pointless.

"Never interrupt your enemy
when he is making a mistake."

"Little strokes fall big oaks."

"Some people walk in the rain, others just get wet."

"Life consists not in holding good cards,
but in playing those you can."

"Don't ever let school
get in the way of your education."

"I have never killed a man, but I have read many
obituaries with great pleasure."
Clarence Darrow

I'm proud of myself. I finished a jigsaw puzzle in 6
months, and the box said 2-4 years.

She's itching for something she won't scratch for.

Why close the barn door after the horses are out?

No more good than an eyeless needle.

Like warming up leftover snow.

Like pushing a wheelbarrow with rope handles.

Like sweet-talking the water out of the well.

So pretty she'd make a man plow through a stump.

She can ride any horse in my string.

"Don't touch" must be one of the scariest things
to read in Braille.

She's built like a brick outhouse.

She's built like a Coke bottle.

She cleans up real nice.

She has more curves than a barrel of snakes.

She's all dressed up like a country bride.

I'd rather watch her walk than eat fried chicken.

Pretty as twelve acres of pregnant red hogs.

A boiled egg is hard to beat.

Cute as a speckled pup under a red wagon.

Finally, a coffee cup for left-handers.

He looks like he was inside the outhouse when the
lightning struck.

She looks like she was born downwind of the outhouse.

So ugly the tide wouldn't take her out.

So ugly his mama had to tie a pork chop around his neck
so the dogs would play with him.

So ugly his mama takes him everywhere she goes
so she doesn't have to kiss him good-bye.

So ugly only his mama loves him—
and she waits till payday.

He got whipped with an ugly stick.

His mama had more hair in the mole on her chin.

Looks like he was pulled through a knothole backwards.

God gives us each a song.
Ute

One finger cannot lift a pebble.
Hopi

70

Remember to set your scales back 10# this week.

Looks like ten miles of bad road.

Looks like he sorts bobcats for a living.

"My mother never saw the irony
in calling me 'a son-of-a-bitch'."
–*Jack Nicholson*

So bowlegged he couldn't catch a pig in a ditch.

I'm not 40-something.
I'm 39.95 plus shipping and handling.

My super power holds onto junk for years
and throws it out a week before I need it.

Ugly as a mud fence.

Ugly as homemade sin.

Ugly as Grandpa's toenails.

He's got a face like the back end of bad luck.

She can't help being ugly, but she could stay home.

He couldn't get a date at the Chicken Ranch
with a truckload of fryers.

Sweeter than stolen honey.

Sweeter than baby's breath.

Sweeter than an old maid's dream.

He took to you like a hog to persimmons.

He took to you like a fish to water.

Happy as a boardinghouse pup.

Happy as a clam at high tide.

Happy as a hog in mud.

Safe as Granny's snuffbox.

Fair to middling.

Went to a flea market…Stole the whole show.

Soft as a two-minute egg.

Funny, I don't remember being absent minded.
Funny, I don't remember being absent minded.

I'm cooking on a front burner today.

If I felt any better,
I'd drop my harp plumb through the cloud.

If I felt any better, I'd think it was a setup.

Some days I feel like a fire hydrant.

I think people my age are much older than I am.

I didn't say he's dumb…I said he chases parked cars.

This is so good it'll make childbirth a pleasure.

Fine as frog fur.

Fine as dollar cotton.

Fine as boomtown silk.

Fine as cream gravy.

The porch light is always burning.

Down the road a piece.

A fur piece.

Turn left past yonder.

I won't say it's far, but I had to grease the wagon twice
before I hit the main road

Two hoots and a holler away.

He's like a blister—
he doesn't show up till the work's all done.

Shy as a mail-order bride.

If it should move and doesn't – Use WD-40
It it does move and shouldn't – Use Duct Tape

Shy as sapphires.

It's scary when you start making the same sounds
as your coffee maker.

Dark as coffin air.

Dark as a pocket.

"He has Van Gogh's ear for music".
–Billy Wilder

I don't know whether I found a rope or lost a horse.

Never trust an atom… They make everything up.

"Measure twice, cut once."

"If you change the way you look at things,
things you look at will change."

Dark as truck-stop coffee

If you put a crouton on your sundae instead of a cherry, it counts as a salad.

Handy as sliced bread.

Handy as shirt pockets.

Handy as a rope at a hanging.

Handy as a latch on the outhouse door

Scarce as hen's teeth.

Scarce as grass around a hog trough.

Scarce as rain barrels.

Scarce as a virgin in a cathouse

Of course I talk to myself... I need expert advice.

It wouldn't cut hot butter.

Twice is what keeps everything from happening at once.

As exciting as waiting for paint to dry.

As exciting as a mashed-potato sandwich.

As much fun as chopping wood.

Simplicity is the essence of creativity.

You say tomato... I say ketchup.

Yesterday is history! Tomorrow is a mystery!
Today is a gift...the Present.

Stop trying to make everyone happy…
You're not Tequila.

Wisdom comes only when you stop looking for it and
start living the life the Creator intended for you.
Hopi

Don't do something permanently stupid
because you're temporarily upset.

It's better to walk alone than in a crowd
going the wrong direction.

"Christmas is a state of mind—Not a date."

If you have to choose between drinking wine everyday
or being skinny, which would you chose, red or white?

"Wine is Earth's answer to the sun."

"No great artist ever sees things as they are."

"When your only tool is a hammer,
every problem looks like a nail."

"One child, one teacher, one pen and one book
can change the world."

Be who you needed when you were younger.

When you forgive, you heal. When you let go, you grow.

If he was dumb as dirt... He could cover about an acre.

Find someone to love and be loved by
and be there in the end to hold their hand.

Forgiveness does not change the past,
but it does enlarge the future.

In a world where you can be anything…be kind!

When you make a commitment, you build hope.
When you keep it, you build trust.

What can a man do that comes close to being a mother?

"May your choices reflect your hopes
and not your fears…"
–Nelson Mandela

The best time to plant a tree was twenty years ago.
The second-best time is now!

Why do we only rest in peace?
Why can't we live in peace too?

"The further a society drifts from the truth,
the more it will hate those who speak it."
–George Orwell

"Regret for wasted time, is more wasted time."

"Denial ain't just a river."
–Mark Twain

"Whatever you do, do it well."
–Walt Disney

"To be who you are, you need to forget
who they told you to be."

"I cook with wine, sometimes I even put it in the food."
–W.C. Fields

"Wine is one of the most civilized things in the world and
one of the most natural things in the world that has been
brought to the greatest perfection, as it offers a greater
range for enjoyment and appreciation than, possibly, any
other purely sensory thing."
–Ernest Hemingway

"Reading the dictionary,
I thought it was a poem about everything."

The Ever-Quotable Yogi Berra

"It's getting late early."

"When you come to the fork in the road… take it."

"You can observe a lot just watching…"

"It ain't over till it's over…"

"It's like déjà vu all over again…"

"No one goes there nowadays… it's too crowded…".

"Baseball is 90% mental and the other half is physical…"

"Nickle ain't worth a dime anymore…"

"Always go to other people's funerals,
otherwise they won't come to yours…"

"We made too many wrong mistakes…"

"Congratulations. I knew the record would stand
until it was broken…"

"You better cut the pizza in four pieces because
I'm not hungry enough to eat six.."

"You wouldn't have won if we'd beaten you…"

"I usually take a two-hour nap from one to four…"

"Never answer an anonymous letter…"

"Slump? I ain't in no slump… I just ain't hitting…"

"How can you think and hit at the same time? …"

"The future ain't what it use to be…"

"I tell the kids, somebody's gotta win,
somebody's gotta lose.
Just don't fight about it. Just try to get better…"

"It gets late early out here…"

"If the people don't want to come out to the ballpark,
nobody's going to stop them…"

"We have deep depth…"

"Pair up in threes..."

"Why buy good luggage?
You only use it when you travel..."

"You've got to be very careful if you don't know where
you are going, because you might not get there..."

"All pitchers are liars or crybabies..."

"Even Napoleon had his Watergate..."

"Bill Dickey is learning me his experience..."

"He hits from both sides of the plate.
He's amphibious..."

"It was impossible to get a conversation going,
everybody was talking too much..."

"I can see how he (Sandy Koufax) won twenty-five
games. What I don't understand is how he lost five..."

"I don't know (if fans running naked across the field
were men or women). They had bags over their heads..."

"I'm a lucky guy and I'm happy to be with the Yankees.
And I want to thank everyone
for making this night necessary..."

"I'm not going to buy my kids an encyclopedia.
Let them walk to school like I did..."

"In baseball, you don't know nothing..."

"I never blame myself when I'm not hitting. I just blame the bat and if it keeps up, I change bats. After all, if I know it isn't my fault that I'm not hitting, how can I get mad at myself"

"I never said most of the things I said..."

"It ain't the heat, it's the humility..."

"If you ask me anything I don't know, I'm not going to answer..."

"I wish everybody had the drive he (Joe DiMaggio) had, He never did anything wrong on the field. I'd never seen him dive for a ball, everything was chest-high catch, and he never walked off the field..."

"So, I'm ugly. I never saw anyone hit with his face..."

(On the 1973 Mets)
"We were overwhelming underdogs..."

"Take it with a grin of salt..."

"The towels were so thick there, I could hardly close my suitcase..."

"Little League baseball is a very good thing because it keeps the parents off the streets..."

"Mickey Mantle was a very good golfer, but we weren't allowed to play golf during the season; only at spring training..."

"You don't have to swing hard to hit a home run. If you got the timing, it'll go..."

"I'm lucky. Usually you're dead to get your own
museum, but I'm still alive to see mine…"

"If I didn't make it in baseball,
I won't have made it workin'. I didn't like to work."

"If the world were perfect, it wouldn't be…"

"A lot of guys go, Hey Yog… say a Yogi-ism. I tell'em. I
don't know any. They want to make one up. I don't make
'em up. I don't even know when I say it. They're the
truth. And it is the truth. I don't know."

<u>Back to the anonymous sources...</u>

I don't judge people based on color,
race religion, sexuality, gender, ability or size...
I base it on whether or not they're an asshole.

Why is abbreviation such a long word?

I started out with nothing. Still have most of it.

Man has responsibility, not power.
Tuscarora

I thought I was wrong once...
I turned out it was a mistake.

Say NO! Then negotiate.

Only dead fish go with the flow.

A vegetarian is a good description of a poor hunter.

There is no cure for curiosity.

Be careful of thoughts...They may become words.

I smile because I know what the hell is going on.

Ham and eggs...A day's work for a chicken.
A lifetime for a pig.

Even a small mouse has anger.
Tribe Unknown

Ever stop to think, then forget to start again?

I have delusions of adequacy.

It's hard to make a comeback
when you haven't been anywhere.

Exercise won't hurt you…But why take a chance?

My finest hour…lasted five minutes.

No river can return to its source,
yet all rivers must have a beginning.
Tribe Unknown

You can tell a lot about a woman…
By the way she's holding a gun.

Ten Miles is a good name for a dog you take for a walk.

A smile is an inexpensive way to improve your looks.

There are no strangers here…
only friends who haven't met.

Teacher said I was late.
I told her class started before I got there.

Fedex and UPS are merging into FedUp.

Sign on the Vet's Office:
"Back in 15 Minutes… Sit… Stay."

My favorite gym activity would be judging.

New Year's resolution…"Not to stab anyone!"

I changed my horn to a gunshot.
People move out of the way faster now.

85

I'd be unstoppable if it wasn't for
physics and law enforcement.

"Canis neus it comedit." My dog ate it.

99% of the lawyers give the rest a good name.

Wrinkled is not one of the things
I want to be when I grow up.

Old age is not as honorable as death,
but most people want it.
Crow

If you see no reason for giving thanks,
the fault lies in yourself.
Minquass

When a clock is hungry...it goes back four seconds.

When she saw her first strands of gray hair
she thought she'd dye.

Acupuncture is a jab well done.

A dentist and a manicurist married.
They fought tooth and nail.

A will is a dead giveaway.

With her marriage, she got a new name and a dress.

Police were called to a Day Care Center where a
three-year-old was resisting a rest.

You can tune a piano, but can't tuna fish.

When fish are in schools, they sometimes take debate.

The guy who fell onto an upholstery machine
is now fully recovered.

If you crossed a cat and a parrot, you'd get a carrot.

Yeah...I'm a little down in the mouth...I ate a duck.

He named his dog "Frost" because he bites.

They named him "Garlic"...
His barks are worst than his bites.

87

Never could dance…two left feet.

Hear about the watch dog that ran in circles?
He needed winding.

Cats are much smarter than dogs.
No way are you going to get eight cats to pull a sleigh
through the snow when it's 20 degrees below zero.

What a life… relaxing without alcohol.

I don't use computers…
I can't stick my head out of Windows 10.

Dogs and men are a lot alike…
they both like to chew wood.

Dogs believe they are human…
Cats believe they are God!

Climb your way to the top…
That's why curtains are there.

The coward shoots with shut eyes.
Oklahoma

It is easy to be brave at a distance.
Omaha

Experience is something you don't get until
just after you need it.

I intend to live forever. So far, so good.

Borrow money from pessimists –
they don't expect it back.

I'd kill for a Nobel Peace Prize.

A hungry stomach makes a short prayer.
Paiute

Half the people you know are below average.

99% of lawyers give the rest a bad name.

82.7% of all statistics are made up on the spot.

A conscience is what hurts
when all your other parts feel so good.

A clear conscience is usually the sign of a bad memory.

If you want the rainbow, you got to put up with the rain.

All those who believe in psychokinesis, raise my hand.

I almost had a psychic girlfriend,
but she left me before we met.

How do you tell when you're out of invisible ink?

If everything seems to be going well,
you have obviously overlooked something.

Depression is merely anger without enthusiasm.

When everything is coming your way,
you're in the wrong lane.

The rain falls on the just and the unjust.
Hopi

Ambition is a poor excuse
for not having enough sense to be lazy.

Eagles may soar,
but weasels don't get sucked into jet engines.

My mechanic told me, "I couldn't repair your brakes,
so I made your horn louder."

Why do psychics have to ask you for your name?

If at first you don't succeed,
destroy all evidence that you tried.

The one who tells the stories rules the world.
Hopi

A conclusion is the place where you got tired of thinking.

The hardness of the butter is proportional
to the softness of the bread.

The problem with the gene pool
is that there is no lifeguard.

The sooner you fall behind,
the more time you'll have to catch up.

The colder the x-ray table,
the more of your body is required to be on it.

Everyone has a photographic memory;
some just don't have film.

If at first you don't succeed, skydiving is not for you.

If your car could travel at the speed of light,
would your headlights work?

Do not argue with an idiot. He will drag you down to his
level and beat you with experience.

"Memory is the diary that we all carry with us."

"Painting is silent poetry
and poetry is painting that speaks."

Everything the power does. It does in a circle.
Lakota Sioux

"Mistakes are always forgivable,
if one has the courage to admit them."

"Knowledge will give you power,
but character will give you respect."

"Make sure your worst enemy
doesn't live between your two ears."

Cherish youth, but trust old age.
Pueblo

A man and woman with many children
have many homes.
Lakota Sioux

I want to die peacefully in my sleep, like my grandfather.
Not screaming and yelling like the passengers in his car.

Going to church doesn't make you a Christian any more
than standing in a garage makes you a car.

The last thing I want to do is hurt you.
But it's still on the list.

Light travels faster than sound.
This is why some people appear bright
until you hear them speak.

Knowledge is knowing a tomato is a fruit;
wisdom is not putting it in a fruit salad.

Evening news is where they begin with 'Good evening',
and then proceed to tell you why it isn't.

A bus station is where a bus stops.
A train station is where a train stops.
On my desk, I have a work station.

How is it one careless match can start a forest fire,
but it takes a whole box to start a campfire?

Some people are like Slinkies...not really good for
anything, but you can't help smiling
when you see one tumble down the stairs.

Dolphins are so smart that within a few weeks of
captivity, they can train people to stand on the very edge
of the pool and throw them fish.

I thought I wanted a career;
turns out I just wanted paychecks.

Whenever I fill out an application, in the part that says "If an emergency, notify:" I put "DOCTOR".

I didn't say it was your fault, I said I was blaming you.

I saw a woman wearing a sweat shirt with "Guess" on it...so I said "Implants?"

Why does someone believe you
when you say there are four billion stars,
but check when you say the paint is wet?

Women will never be equal to men until they can walk down the street with a bald head and a beer gut, and still think they are sexy.

Why do Americans choose from just two people to run for President and 50 for Miss America?

Behind every successful man is his woman.
Behind the fall of a successful man
is usually another woman.

A clear conscience is usually the sign of a bad memory.

You do not need a parachute to skydive.
You only need a parachute to skydive twice.

The voices in my head may not be real,
but they have some good ideas!

Hospitality: making your guests feel like they're at home, even if you wish they were.

"I've had a perfectly wonderful evening.
But, this wasn't it."
Groucho Marx

"As I ate oysters with their strong taste of the sea and
their faint metallic taste that the cold white wine washed
away, leaving only the sea taste and the succulent texture,
and as I drank their cold liquid from each shell and
washed it down with the crisp taste of wine,
I lost the empty feeling
and began to be happy and make plans."
–*Ernest Hemingway*

I discovered I scream the same way whether I'm about to
be devoured by a great white shark
or if a piece of seaweed touches my foot.

There's a fine line between cuddling and holding
someone down so they can't get away.

I always take life with a grain of salt,
plus a slice of lime and a shot of tequila.

When tempted to fight fire with fire,
remember that the Fire Department usually uses water.

You're never too old to learn something stupid.

To be sure of hitting the target, shoot first
and call whatever you hit the target.

Some people hear voices. Some see invisible people.
Others have no imagination whatsoever.

A bus is a vehicle that runs twice as fast
when you are after it as when you are in it.

If you are supposed to learn from your mistakes,
why do some people have more than one child?

Change is inevitable, except from a vending machine.

"Where there's a will, I want to be in it."

We never really grow up,
we only learn how to act in public.

War does not determine who is right - only who is left.

Fear is a reaction. Courage is a decision.

CONFUCIUS NEARLY SAID

Man who wants pretty nurse must be patient.

Man who loose key to girls apartment, get no new key.

Passionate kiss, like spider web, leads to undoing of fly.

Lady who goes camping must beware of evil intent.

Squirrel who runs up woman's leg will not find nuts.

Man who leaps off cliff jumps to conclusion.

Man who eats many prunes get good run for money.

Man says stomach is flat… "l" is silent.

Man who fight with wife all day, get no peace at night.

Man who drives like hell is bound to get there.

Man who lives in glass house
should change clothes in basement.

Mountain Humor Signs

I'M FRIENDS WITH 25 LETTERS OF
THE ALPHABET
I DON'T KNOW Y

COW STUMBLES INTO A POT FIELD!
THE STEAKS HAVE NEVER BEEN
HIGHER

CRUSHING POP CANS
IS SODA PRESSING

IN SEARCH OF FRESH VEGETABLE
PUNS ?
LETTUCE KNOW

HE WHO LAUGHS LAST
DIDN'T GET IT

BIG SHOUT OUT TO ALL MY FINGERS
I CAN ALWAYS COUNT ON THEM

REMEMBER IF THE WORLD DIDN'T
SUCK
WE'D ALL FALL OFF

IRONY,
THE OPPOSITE OF WRINGLY

TRIED TO GRAB THE FOG
I MIST

MY REALITY CHECK BOUNCED

WHAT IF I TOLD YOU
YOU READ THE TOP LINE WRONG

IF YOU SUCK AT PLAYING THE
TRUMPET
THAT'S PROBABLY WHY

BAN PRE-SHREDDED CHEESE
MAKE AMERICA GRATE AGAIN

ELECTRICIANS HAVE TO STRIP
TO MAKE ENDS MEET

FOR CHEMISTS ALCOHOL IS NOT A
PROBLEM
IT'S A SOLUTION

MY MOOD RING IS MISSING AND I
DON'T KNOW HOW TO FEEL ABOUT
IT

I SCREAM…YOU SCREAM…
THE POLICE COME…IT'S AWKWARD

I LIKE COOKING MY FAMILY AND MY
PETS
USE COMMAS, THEY SAVE LIVES

DESPITE THE HIGH COST OF LIVING
IT REMAINS POPULAR

THE PROBLEM WITH POLITICAL
JOKES
IS THAT THEY SOMETIMES GET
ELECTED

WISHING YOU A HAPPY
WHATEVER DOESN'T OFFEND YOU

DOGS CAN'T OPERATE MRI
SCANNERS
BUT CATSCAN

OUR MOUNTAINS AREN'T JUST
FUNNY
THEY'RE HILL AREAS

TURNING VEGAN WOULD BE
A BIG MISSED STEAK

WELL TO BE FRANK
I'D HAVE TO CHANGE MY NAME

WHENEVER I TRY TO EAT HEALTHY
A CHOCOLATE BAR LOOKS AT ME
AND SNICKERS

LIFE IS SHORT. IF YOU CAN'T LAUGH
AT YOUSELF CALL ME, I WILL

Seattle Propane Signs

FROG PARKING ONLY
ALL OTHERS WILL BE TOAD

ANTS ARE HEALTHY BECAUSE
THEY HAVE LITTLE ANTIBODIES

IS THERE EVER A DAY
THAT MATTRESSES ARE NOT FOR
SALE?

WENT TO THE AIR & SPACE MUSEUM
BUT THERE WAS NOTHING THERE

HOLD THE DOOR OPEN FOR A CLOWN
IT'S A NICE JESTER

I'M STILL HOT.
IT JUST COMES IN FLASHES NOW

I CHILD PROOFED MY HOUSE
BUT THE KIDS STILL GIT IN

IF ATTACKED BY A MOB OF CLOWNS
GO FOR THE JUGGLER

I WANT TO GROW MY OWN FOOD
BUT I CAN'T FIND BACON SEEDS

I JUST DID A WEEK WORTH OF
CARDIO…AFTER WALKING INTO A
SPIDER WEB

ABSTINENCE IS A GOOD THING
IF PRACTICED IN MODERATION

IF YOUR CAR IS RUNNING
I'M VOTING FOR IT

THIS IS MY STEP LADDER
I NEVER KNEW MY REAL LADDER

MY WIFE SAID I NEVER LISTEN TO
HER OR SOMETHING LIKE THAT

The Washington Post's **Mensa Invitational** once again invited readers to take any word from the dictionary, alter it by adding, subtracting, or changing one letter, and supply a new definition.

Here are the winners:

1. **Cashtration** (n.): The act of buying a house, which renders the subject financially impotent for an indefinite period of time.

2. **Ignoranus**: A person who's both stupid and an asshole.

3. **Intaxicaton**: Euphoria at getting a tax refund, which lasts until you realize it was your money to start with.

4. **Reintarnation**: Coming back to life as a hillbilly.

5. **Bozone** (n.): The substance surrounding stupid people that stops bright ideas from penetrating. The bozone layer, unfortunately, shows little sign of breaking down in the near future.

6. **Foreploy**: Any misrepresentation about yourself for the purpose of getting laid.

7. **Giraffiti**: Vandalism spray-painted very, very high.

8. **Sarchasm**: The gulf between the author of sarcastic wit and the person who doesn't get it.

9. **Inoculatte**: To take coffee intravenously when you are running late.

10. **Osteopornosis**: A degenerate disease. (*This one got extra credit.*)

11. **Karmageddon**: It's like, when everybody is sending off all these really bad vibes, right? And then, like, the Earth explodes and it's like, a serious bummer.

12. **Decafalon** (n.): The grueling event of getting through the day consuming only things that are good for you.

13. **Glibido**: All talk and no action.

14. **Dopeler Effect**: The tendency of stupid ideas to seem smarter when they come at you rapidly.

15. **Arachnoleptic Fit** (n.): The frantic dance performed just after you've accidentally walked through a spider web.

16. **Beelzebug** (n.): Satan in the form of a mosquito, that gets into your bedroom at three in the morning and cannot be cast out.

17. **Caterpallor** (n.): The color you turn after finding half a worm in the fruit you're eating.

"Mo, it takes a very narrow mind to only spell a word one way!"

The Washington Post has also published the winning submissions to its yearly contest, in which readers are asked to supply alternate meanings for common words.

And the winners are:
1. **Coffee**, n. The person upon whom one coughs.

2. **Flabbergasted**, adj. Appalled by discovering how much weight one has gained.

3. **Abdicate**, v. To give up all hope of ever having a flat stomach.

4. **Esplanade**, v. To attempt an explanation while drunk.

5. **Willy-nilly**, adj. Impotent.

6. **Negligent**, adj. Absentmindedly answering the door when wearing only a nightgown.

7. **Lymph**, v. To walk with a lisp.

8. **Gargoyle**, n. Olive-flavored mouthwash.

9. **Flatulence**, n. Emergency vehicle that picks up someone who has been run over by a steamroller.

10. **Balderdash**, n. A rapidly receding hairline.

11. **Testicle**, n. A humorous question on an exam.

12. **Rectitude**, n. The formal, dignified bearing adopted by proctologists.

13. **Pokemon**, n. A Rastafarian proctologist.

14. **Oyster**, n. A person who sprinkles his conversation with Yiddishisms.

15. **Frisbeetarianism**, n. The belief that, after death, the soul flies up onto the roof and gets stuck there.

16. **Circumvent**, n. An opening in the front of boxer shorts worn by Jewish men.

BOSS' favorite
CRAB BAIT & HAIRBALL APHORISMS

*"In ancient times, cats were worshipped as Gods—
HAIRBALL has never forgotten that."*

"The average dog is nicer than the average person."

"A cat does not offer services, the cat offers itself."

*"CRAB BAIT comes when he is called...
HAIRBALL will take a message and get back to you."*

"CRAB BAIT does speak, but only to those who listen."

*"You can teach HAIRBALL to do anything
that he wants to do."*

"Dogs never lie about love."

"Family is the best thing you could ever wish for."

*"Meow is like "Aloha" to HAIRBALL...
It can mean anything."*

"Some angels choose fur instead of wings."

*"Cats are like music; It is foolish to try to explain
their worth to those who don't appreciate them."*

"Every puppy should have a boy."

*"It's not <u>what</u> we have in life,
but <u>who</u> we have in our lives that matters."*

"If cats could talk... they wouldn't."

"CRAB BAIT lives like the gate is always open!"

"You want me to purr... I charge extra for that."

*"A black cat crossing your path
signifies that it is going somewhere."*

"Be the person your dog thinks you are."

*"Never forget who was there for you
when no one else was"*

*"People who hate cats
will come back as mice in their next lives."*

*"Life is not how fast you run or how high you climb,
but how well you bounce."*

"HAIRBALL is a connoisseur of comfort."

"Dogs have masters, Cats have staff."

*"I gave up trying to understand people long ago...
Now I let them try to understand me."*

"Hand over the catnip, and no one gets hurt."

"Women and HAIRBALL will do as they please."

*"Life is sunshine and rain... (That makes rainbows);
It's days and nights; It's peaks and valleys."*

"Who cares what others think?"

*"Worrying won't stop the bad stuff from happening.
It just stops you from enjoying the good."*

110

"Everyone thinks they have the best dog,
and none of them are wrong."

"Boss should have named me 'Rolex'.
Then if I didn't turn out to be a good bird dog,
I would be his watch dog."

"Blood makes you related... Love makes you a family."

"Life is the little things."

"Our home is blessed with love, laughter, friendship and
CRAB BAIT, HAIRBALL, MO & DIRT."

"We really do THANK YOU for reading our book.
You can order copies for your family and friends from
Amazon.com and CRAB-BAIT.com

Made in the USA
San Bernardino, CA
22 December 2018